OLIVIER!

This is your Time!

Avoiding the

Critical Mistakes

...That Will Short-Circuit Your Career!

by G. Eric Gordon

Foreword by
Steve Gilliland
author of *Enjoy The Ride* and *Mum's The Word*

**PEARHOUSE
PRESS**

Published by Pearhouse Press, Inc., Pittsburgh, PA 15208
www.pearhousepress.com

Printed in the United States of America
ISBN: 978-0-9802355-1-7

Cover Design and Book Layout: Mike Murray, Pearhouse Productions

Table of Contents

Stop Where You Are!

I'M WRITING THIS BOOK, *Avoiding the Eight Critical Mistakes…That Will Short-Circuit Your Career,* because I have a great passion and need to help anyone who is floundering in his or her career. If I had approached my early opportunities with the knowledge I'll share with you in this book, I may never have become a consultant. This is because I would be too busy enjoying a tremendously successful career as a hospital CEO!

I've written this book to help you go as high as your ambitions and talents can take you, in any corporation or organization. Just *avoid* doing some of the stupid things (so many) people do (me included) to mess themselves up. *The key is to know that problems you experience in your professional life are created (at least partially) by you!* Take responsibility for your actions, and your career. This approach will assist you in avoiding the critical mistakes we'll discuss in this book.

The framework of the book, is simple, yet powerful, and easy to apply and will yield positive results for you. So let's get started now. You can read this book in one sitting. Then, read it again! Most importantly, be *determined to take action* on the principles and strategies discussed in this book. There is no power where there is no action!

Hey, relax! This will be a fun read for you. I've already made most of the mistakes (which is why I do what I do). All you have to do is *learn, act,* and *profit* from them. Then pass the book on to a colleague you appreciate. Enjoy!

G. Eric Gordon, Author

P.S. To all my former bosses: I finally got it!

Foreword

WHEN G. ERIC GORDON ASKED ME to write a foreword for *Avoiding the Eight Critical Mistakes*, I said I would be most honored to do so. After reading the manuscript, I'm especially honored. I love the book!

Avoiding the Eight Critical Mistakes stimulated my mind, reminding me that any individual can achieve more if he or she can avoid making some bad choices—especially in these increasingly complex and changing times. It also reminded me that if I could have anything in the world, I believe I would choose wisdom. For, you see, wisdom is the art of living. If we learn how to live, if we develop the craftsmanship of making a life, then we'll have everything we've ever wanted and ever needed.

In a day when the world culture is rapidly falling apart, we desperately need to learn how to lead and live. Beyond that we'll have a life of great success and true significance. That's what this book is all about. Eric spent years in leadership and among leaders to find out what were the non-negotiables that were true in their lives that enabled them to not only make a great living but to have a successful life and lifestyle.

Even more impressive, the book is a blueprint for management and could be a required course in business and management schools. Nothing is more important than leadership—in general, and particularly in confusing times like these. And in my view, G. Eric Gordon has done a great job of revealing mistakes that will short-circuit your career. Eric is a colleague, so this could be seen as a self-serving introduction. Problem is, I hold my friends and colleagues to a much higher standard than others. I informed Eric I would not write this foreword unless I "love the book." Moreover, I have the advantage of having observed him, hands dirty, working with hundreds of client leaders on the slippery topic of leading—with peerless results. This is to say that every idea in this book has successfully withstood the test of real people—and very real feedback.

Yes, Eric: *I love this book*. The personal accounts are inspiring. The ideas are time tested. Not only are the ideas "right on," but they fill a gaping void in leadership literature. Plus, the timing is right. From the world of corporation to the world of Washington, D.C., understanding these critical mistakes that need to be avoided can move mountains for would-be leaders who are determined to connect, inspire and make a difference.

If we are to survive and thrive in the twenty-first century, learning to avoid these eight critical mistakes is a must. This book could easily become the "Professional's Success Manual." Besides reading this book, I see this evolving into a must-attend workshop for every person who aspires to be in leadership.

Let me leave you with the words of America's dean of psychology, William James. He suggests three steps to take if you honestly want to change: start immediately, start flamboyantly, and make no excuses. Eric will help you recognize the barriers to being successful, but it will be up to you whether or not you are willing to change and avoid mistakes that will inhibit your growth.

I hope your journey brings you to the places found in your fondest dreams. The possibilities for a better life are out there and waiting for you. They are within your grasp. You have taken the first step to *Avoiding the Eight Critical Mistakes*—you are reading this book. Life is a banquet. Sample its goodness. Strive to be more and better. You can do it. Life is a gift. Enjoy The Ride!

Steve Gilliland
Author of "Enjoy The Ride" and "Mum's The Word"

5

Avoiding the

8

Critical Mistakes

...That Will Short-Circuit Your Career!

1

My Boss Is a Jerk

IT SEEMS LIKE EVERYONE I KNOW has some kind of issue with his or her boss. This phenomenon is as old as work itself. Fred Flintstone never appreciated Mr. Slate. Dagwood never understood Mr. Dithers. And George Jetson never had anything good to say about Mr. Spacely! The list goes on. Did I mention Beetle Bailey and the Sarge?

Disrespecting and often disliking the boss is the first and, often, most critical mistake we make. Many of us see the boss as an enemy. The boss should be your greatest ally! Whenever people are in the mood to complain about their jobs, most start with their bosses. Bosses are the most reviled members of the work team. Bosses are criticized for being lazy, too strict, too lenient, anal retentive, clueless and whatever else you're currently thinking.

I also suffered from this kind of craziness. I made the boss into an enemy at almost every job I had. I was critical, distant and suspicious. I would become nervous or agitated whenever the boss would come into my work area. If the boss wanted to know what was going on within my department, I would get defensive and wonder why I was being "checked on." Whenever the boss would give me criticism, I would immediately become resentful and take the feedback personally. Ridiculous!

I hope this book will help to eliminate this kind of stupidity within the work place. Yes, there are plenty of bad bosses out there. Yes, they can be bullies and often mistreat employees. But most "good" bosses want to get the work done and empower their staffers. This, of course, can lead to increased opportunities for the boss and others associated with his achievements.

The first key to achieving success within any job or career opportunity is to develop a solid (great?) relationship with your boss. A good relationship with your boss can lead to many opportunities, including increased responsibilities, promotion and growth opportunities. Frankly, I'm stating the obvious when I tell you that your boss can make your work life productive and profitable, or she can make the job seem like a "living hell." Remember, bosses are people, too. I'm not joking! They require what all of us want and desire—respect, appreciation and admiration. This is where we'll begin the critical task of building a tremendous relationship with your boss/supervisor/leader.

The following traits must be present to establish a good relationship. This provides a good foundation for you and your boss.

- ✔ Trust and Honesty
- ✔ Appreciation and Respect
- ✔ Open Communication
- ✔ Ability to Empathize

Read on! The information that follows will enable you to create a fabulous working relationship with the person who is critical to your success. At the *very least*, these strategies will allow you to improve almost any relationship. There are three major components to our "winning relationships" formula—appreciate the boss's successes, focus on the boss's priorities and give loyalty and respect.

1. Appreciate the Boss's Successes

For many, complimenting the boss is as painful as having a tooth pulled without novocaine. Your boss has achieved at *least* one level higher than your current position, so why not discuss his successes? Talk to the boss about his journey, the obstacles he had to overcome, the people who helped him along the way, the mistakes he made and, most importantly, the lessons he learned. View your relationship as an opportunity to learn how to succeed within the organization. Your boss is in a position to be an ideal mentor for your future success. Take these steps:

a. **Watch and observe the decisions made by your boss.** What are the factors that influence them? What impact is she attempting to achieve, and for whom? What worked or is working well? How would you have responded to the same situation?

b. **Observe your boss under pressure.** How well does he "think on his feet"? How well does he manage or control their emotions?

c. **Ask questions.** For example, what makes your boss successful—education, preparation, information, determination? Discuss your thoughts with her.

d. **Ask your boss to provide you with feedback regarding ways you could be more successful.** Ask him to provide information on your areas of strength and how you can apply your talents. Also ask for feedback, outlining areas needing improvement. Focus on improvements for future growth and opportunities within your organization.

e. **Finally, discuss your goals and career objectives with your boss.** Get her honest assessment of your chances for promotion and what else you could do to grow your career. Your boss can be your greatest ally.

Ask your questions with sincerity, and they will be answered. Your boss can be an advocate to help springboard your career to greatness. Remember, bosses are like everyone else. They like to hear about their own accomplishments and be appreciated for their successes. Don't wait. Take an interest in your boss today.

2. Focus On the Boss's Priorities

This is the most critical step you'll take in this process. Your *first* priority at work should be to learn what your boss wants and expects. Build your work schedule and processes to meet the needs of your first and most important customer! Many of us may feel that we do this, but this is *the* most critical step in establishing a solid relationship with your boss. Follow these steps:

a. **Ask your boss about his "vision" for your department.** What are his hopes and goals for the future?

b. **Ask your boss about which activities and processes she feels are most critical for achieving her/the company's**

objectives. Ask her to identify the "Top Three" priorities for your area.

c. **Ask your boss what success "looks like," relating to his top priorities or to any work assignment.** Have him identify performance goals or success targets he desires to achieve.

d. **Clarify your boss's desires, then inform her about how you will achieve her objectives or address her concerns.** Also tell your boss when she can expect to see the results she desires. You should also discuss contingencies and other factors that could negatively impact your ability to achieve the results she desires.

e. **Provide your boss with regular progress reports and updates.** Be proactive with information your boss deems important.

These actions will help your boss to see *you* as a valuable resource and ally. People, your boss included, appreciate anyone who they feel is committed to helping them achieve higher degrees or levels of success. A consistent trait of human relations is "reciprocity." Anytime you do something for someone else, the other person feels almost obligated to do something back for you! When you consistently help your boss achieve his goals, your boss, in time, will see it as his duty to return something good to you. Most importantly, this step will build confidence and demonstrate your commitment to your boss's success.

3. Give Loyalty and Respect

It's amazing how these words always seem to be missing when it comes to our relationship with our bosses. Many are quick to complain about the boss's shortcomings. Just remember, your boss made one good professional decision in her career: she hired you! If this is not the case, if you were actually hired by someone else, it's okay. The boss *retained* you and still wants to have confidence in you. Follow these steps:

a. **Never publicly "bad mouth" your boss or his decisions.** Don't whine, gripe or moan. Focus on what *you* control and what *you* can do to make a situation better.

b. **Anytime you are unhappy or have a disagreement with your boss, always take your concern directly to her.** Try to communicate your concern as an "opportunity" that you are looking forward to tackling or assisting with.

c. **Be honest with your boss if you feel he is off base or making a poor decision.** Have observations, documentation and data to support your contentions.

d. **Remind your boss of your commitment to her.** Tell her how important the relationship is to you and how hard you'll work to see that her objectives are achieved.

NOTE: If you cannot respect or appreciate your boss because your boss is dishonest, lacks integrity or is morally corrupt, then you must *leave the employment ASAP.* You are under no obligation to honor or support anyone who lies, cheats, steals or lacks integrity.

These three steps will allow you to expand, broaden and strengthen your relationship with your boss. Be proactive about your relationship with your boss. Appreciate your boss's achievements. Spend time with your boss and ask questions about his priorities and his mission. Give respect and loyalty to your boss. Also, take it easy and never take your boss's criticism personally. When disagreements occur, getting mad will only make matters worse. Control your emotions and focus on fixing problems and producing more than expected. These steps will allow you to create a tremendous relationship with your boss and help you secure and stabilize your work experience. Begin using these techniques right away, and start gaining the benefits that come from working with an ally!

Note To Bosses!

Yes, it is vitally important for staffers to have appreciation and respect for you. However, *your actions* will determine whether you will keep their respect. If you desire to grow greater respect and credibility consistently, work to create value for your staff members. Respect them as colleagues and work to grow their skills as professionals. Above all else, always conduct business with the highest level of honesty, integrity and accountability. Here's a story from Ms. Arquila Todd, a colleague who is a QA manager for a Federal Agency:

LACKING ACCOUNTABILITY!

On June 15th my boss went on a two-and-a-half-week vacation and left me in charge of the QA office. Our office is responsible for auditing departments within our organization. I was prepared because I had taken on that responsibility prior to my boss leaving for vacation. I had spoken with a subject matter expert who was going to assist me with the audit of our *training department*. We set the date, and the stage was set for the training department's audit to be conducted on Monday, June 19th. The Thursday prior to the audit, I checked with my expert regarding the time we would start. He was unavailable, so I left a message. On Friday at 2:15 pm (fifteen minutes before I left the office), I received a call from my expert. He told me that he'd been informed that the audit had been rescheduled for July 10th. Who notified him of the changes? That's right—my boss!

Well, you would think someone would find it in their hearts to tell *me, the person doing the audit!* But no, I get this information from someone at the service area, *not* my boss, who works in the same building with me! Incredible!

I was really outdone because I had taken so much time to prepare for the audit. I felt compelled to speak to my boss about his not mentioning the new date to me (accountability!) When he called to check on the office, I told him how I had learned about the new date and mentioned that it would have been nice of him to share the new date with me since he and the chief had changed it. He said the chief was the person who should have told me. He knew he could have contacted me personally (as he had my expert), since I was *his* representative in charge of processes that impact the reputation of *his* department. What's sad is that this is typical of how he handles things. These repeated occurrences have resulted in my losing trust and confidence in him. I no longer believe he'll "do the right thing."

– Ms. Arquila Todd, Government Employee

So, bosses, be accountable and reliable and conduct business with the highest level of integrity if you want to avoid agitation and discontentment among your staff members and within your organizations.

THOUGHTS

1. *I've identified a talent or strength my boss possesses. I've also identified what I appreciate about my boss's management style.*

2. *I've met with my boss and have identified his/her top priorities.*

3. *I keep my boss informed about how my work or projects are progressing. I also inform my boss about the expected benefits of my actions.*

4. *I am proactive about resolving problems and finding solutions to anticipated contingencies.*

5. *Here are a few ways I demonstrate commitment and loyalty to my boss:*

_____

_____

_____

_____

_____

_____

6. *I compliment my boss regularly.*

2

No One Understands, Likes or Appreciates Me

DOES IT EVER FEEL as if you're *all alone?* Like you're an alien on a lost and distant planet with no one there who understands you or knows what you're thinking or wanting? Well, you may feel as though you're alone, but you actually have a lot in common with the great majority of the human race. Most people will go through periods of loneliness, rejection, depression and lost self-esteem. Unfortunately, many wallow in this condition and actually magnify these feeling of loneliness while at work.

How many times have you heard people make statements like these?

- ✓ I don't like anyone who works here.
- ✓ These people get on my nerves.
- ✓ These people just don't get it.
- ✓ Most of our team members are simply a bunch of back stabbers, etc., etc.

Actually, the *no-one-understands-likes-or-appreciates-me* mistake could easily be *the* greatest mistake of our careers and within our lives. Why? Our ability to have healthy relationships is directly affected by our self-esteem. The great majority of relationship problems are a result of negative self-esteem and unhealthy self-images. It is estimated that humans spend over 95 percent of their waking hours thinking about *themselves.* Unfortunately, if we have low self-esteem, we tend to focus on problems within our lives and work environment instead of the opportunities present.

Each of us perceives the world through a set of filters. We use these filters to determine what's right, fair and just. Normally, our perception of the world is consistent with our own self-concept. If we like and feel good about ourselves, then we tend to like and feel good about others. Most importantly, we expect others to feel good about us, too. But if we have negative feelings toward ourselves, we tend to see the negative in others and look at others with suspicion. In fact, if you suffer from low self-esteem, you feel that virtually everyone is a threat to you.

I can honestly say that my failure to develop quality relationships with bosses and others, in and out of work, was due to my low self-esteem. I didn't feel good about myself. I often felt alone, left out and misunderstood. My low self-esteem increased my feelings of negativity, isolation and selfishness. As a result, I seldom sought guidance, help or assistance from others. Almost *all* of the "Critical Mistakes" can be traced to low self-esteem. My low self-esteem led to the following negative perceptions:

1. I always took any kind of criticism personally and negatively. I believed "they" were out to get me. I felt like a victim. I alienated my boss and others.

2. I limited my contribution, input, passions and commitment to the team. How could I give to others when I was so focused on myself (and how bad I had it)? I was too worried about what others were doing to me to think about how I could *actually serve* others.

3. I also lowered my expectations for success. Feeling alienated affected my morale and confidence and hindered my decision-making.

Studies show that all of us suffer from some level or degree of low self-esteem. Take the first step necessary in creating successful outcomes for yourself and others by developing a healthy self-esteem.

Follow the steps listed below and get to work.

1. Know, Accept and Appreciate Yourself

Self-help Gurus Jack Canfield and Brian Tracy tell us that a healthy self-concept and feelings of self-acceptance are necessary for high achievement. *Why?* Because we can rise only to the level of our own self-image. So, to raise your level of achievement, consider the following strategies to raise the level of your esteem and self-concept.

a. **Mental house cleaning**. Immediately begin listing all the negative and self-limiting beliefs you have about yourself. Reject old, outdated, negative concepts. Throw them out or take action to change them. Create and nurture new beliefs and habits. Begin by making a few lists:

✓ List the talents and skills that make you distinctive or different.

✓ List your accomplishments or things you are proud of.

✓ Create a set of values that you respect and appreciate and incorporate them into your life. Then practice living *your* values. What values are most important to you? List the things you value most in life.

✓ Practice being decent and polite to others. Demonstrate goodwill.

b. **Reaffirm yourself daily with self-talk**. Give yourself daily reminders to build your confidence and enthusiasm. Your self-talk should remind you of your strengths and abilities to overcome hardships and adversity. They should be present-tensed, short, positive statements that lift your confidence and spirit.

2. Have Confidence and Integrity

The foundation of high self-esteem is a belief within ourselves that we are people of quality and worthy of all the success we can achieve. If you are filled with guilt, self-loathing or self-pity, you'll feel unworthy of success. Ultimately, you *expect* to fail.

a. **Begin with integrity**. Integrity stands for honor and trustworthiness. Integrity says "I mean what I say, and I say what I mean." Begin by telling the truth. It's amazing how many people find it hard to tell the truth. You'll also be amazed at how empowered and free you'll feel. Here are some things to think about:

✓ Whenever you're about to give a comment or opinion, always ask yourself, "Is it true?"

✓ Tell your friends and associates of your determination to build integrity. Ask them to practice the same concept when dealing with you.

✓ Ask yourself daily, "How are my actions promoting integrity?"

✓ Practice, practice, practice. It's not easy being a person of honor today. This is why you'll have tremendous appreciation for yourself once you consistently practice integrity.

b. **Develop unshakable confidence**. Confidence is necessary for any worthwhile achievement. Confidence keeps your expectations for success high. It strengthens your beliefs and determination to succeed. There are strategies you can take to build your confidence.

✓ Know you are good. You must have some talent or skill to feel confident. Demonstrating high levels of job knowledge and competence will help you solve more work problems. The more problems we solve at work, the more problems we'll expect to solve. This feeds our feelings of self-worth due to our ability to create more value.

✓ Live with values and integrity. We discussed this earlier. Focus on the legacy you hope to build and ultimately leave.

✓ Have respect for failure. Fear robs us of the confidence necessary to take action. Lose your *fear* of failure and you grow in your ability to take action. Remember, we learn from failure, so failure is a good thing. As you overcome your fear, you'll achieve more of your goals and your confidence will grow. In a short time, you'll become unstoppable.

✓ <u>Perseverance and determination</u>. Toughen your approach and be determined to never quit. The more you are able to stay the course, the greater your chance of achieving your goals.

Ego and lack of integrity destroyed a great consulting opportunity and my relationship with a potentially great mentor. In the year 2000 my consulting business was booming. I had a couple of large contracts with major firms, and opportunities were raining down on me. During this time, I completed some leadership training with the staff at a Houston-area Medical Center. The training went over so well that the CEO asked me to sign a contract to provide coaching sessions for his department directors—this was *great!* We agreed on a price and timelines, and within months I had started the sessions. I quickly realized that not every director was interested in my coaching or even wanted my help or advice. In short, a few rejected me. What did I do? Well, instead of finding new or different ways to communicate with them, I alienated them. My ego took over, and I stopped trying to help a few of them. To add insult to injury, during our final session, I had a party and gave out trophies (but only to those directors who "allowed me" to help them. I also did another stupid thing. While working at the hospital, I was contacted by another hospital system looking for a consultant to audit their Human Resources department and provide some staff training. Well, as a contractor, I wanted the job. Unfortunately, my experience in HR made auditing the department impossible. So I approached the HR Director at the Medical Center where I was coaching and asked if she would like to do some "free-lance consulting" with my firm and earn some extra money. I later learned that this action could have been perceived as a breach of ethics (even though at the time I did not think I had done anything wrong). I believe the HR Director went and told the CEO. The CEO never mentioned it directly, but he became cold and distant. During our out-briefing, he told me that every success was dependent upon one thing: integrity. He then handed me a book on leadership integrity. I was never invited back! Another hard "lesson learned."

3. Market Yourself and Your Talents

It's a mistake to whine and complain that others don't understand or appreciate you. Most of the time, people are too busy thinking about their problems to concern themselves with yours. Stay confident and create a system for marketing yourself. Don't be put off by the term *marketing*. Marketing is simply a way to educate and inform others about your skills, talents, experience and abilities. Marketing describes your way of doing business. It allows you to inform others of actions and/or solutions you can bring to a situation or circumstance. Consider the following as a guide to marketing yourself.

a. **Build yourself**. First, inform your associates/colleagues/supervisor of talents, achievements and/or exceptional skills that have made you successful.

✓ Let others know how you'll handle their concern or complaint.

✓ Inform them of the steps involved with the process and the timelines associated with each step.

✓ Address any contingencies that may hamper your progress.

✓ Communicate your commitment to helping them achieve their performance goals.

✓ Be consistent. Follow through on assigned tasks and obligations.

b. **Be a difference maker**. Focus on exceeding expectations and creating more value. By creating more value for others, others will value you more! This will enhance your credibility and reputation as a producer and problem solver. Every success in life begins with a commitment to serve and enhance the lives of others. In time, you'll become unstoppable!

THOUGHTS AND QUESTIONS TO CONSIDER

1. *What do you like or appreciate most about yourself?*

2. *What are your greatest talents or strengths?*

3. *What affirmations have you developed to keep you focused and positive?*

4. *How are you demonstrating a commitment to integrity?*

5. *What actions will you take to develop "Unshakable Confidence"?*

SAMPLE AFFIRMATIONS (OR SELF-TALK)

✓ *"I am smart, capable and confident."*

✓ *"I am well-prepared and excited about this opportunity."*

✓ *"I always expect to come out on top."*

✓ *"I'm hard to beat. I'm flexible and quick to respond to my customer's needs."*

✓ *"I really enjoy my work."*

✓ *"Every day I grow smarter, stronger and more determined."*

It's Not My Fault!

MOST PEOPLE WHO FAIL, OR THOSE WHO WALLOW in mediocrity (me included), make the critical mistake of **failing to take responsibility!** They constantly blame others for their mistakes, poor judgment and bad decisions. I had few administrative skills and poor work habits, yet I always felt my failures were due to someone else. I never felt *I* had done anything wrong. "It's Not *My* Fault," I would whine when confronted about poor decisions or outcomes.

I once heard Ross Schafer say, "Success is your own fault!" You must be totally responsible for your success or failure. This begins with performing your responsibilities and duties at the highest levels of excellence. Let's begin by recognizing the mistakes that lead to ineffective, inefficient and incompetent outcomes.

The key to creating a successful career lies in our ability to win and keep the trust of our bosses and employers. If your manager trusts and believes in you, she will give you important, career-enhancing duties and assignments. The more success you have in completing these tasks, *the greater your perceived value,* which, of course, leads to *more* important assignments and *more* responsibility and *more* money! I think you understand where this is going. The success formula for eliminating the *it's-not-my-fault* mistake is truly this simple:

**Perform Task & Achieve Desired Result =
Greater Responsibility / Position / Salary, etc.**

Successful professionals begin by taking responsibility. This chapter will outline the six important strategies you'll need for taking responsibility, allowing you to create the successful outcomes you desire.

1. Know What You Do Well

The first step you must take is to understand where (or what) your professional strengths are. When are you most productive? What types of projects or tasks stimulate you to do your best work? Where do your talents and interests lie? When do you struggle to complete tasks? Where can you get better? What skills or talents would you like / need to strengthen?

While working at a hospital in Dallas, Texas, I was approached by our Chief Financial Officer (CFO). He wanted to know if I had ever written a business plan. He was looking for someone with skills in that area to write one for the new laundry service the hospital planned to open soon. The CFO was excited because the new laundry system would have so much capacity that he was hoping to market laundry services to neighboring hospitals. I told him that I did have "some experience" with business plans and that I was certain I could write one for the linen service. This was a mistake! Not only had I *never* written a business plan, I had never even seen a completed one. As you might have guessed, my business plan was a disaster! It looked worse than some college student's term paper. It lacked critical information and data that decision makers would need to adequately market and manage the new linen service. After reviewing the plan, the CFO basically threw the failed document out. He was very unhappy with the poor quality of my work (particularly the cost projections per lb./laundry) and mentioned this to my supervisor.

Lesson: I should have been honest with the CFO from the beginning. I should have told him that I had no idea how to write a business plan, then told him, however, that I'd be happy to research how it might be done. This way, if he still decided to give the project to me, his expectations (and criticisms) would have been reduced because of to my lack of experience in that area. Instead, I wasted everyone's time for months trying to figure out the best way to complete a project that was doomed to fail. I simply did not have the skills or experience. So, know what you do well, and speak honestly about your limitations as well as your talents and experiences.

2. Establish Clear Expectations or Results

Have you ever worked hard on a project and turned it in on time to your boss, only to have it turned inside out and returned to you as something totally foreign to the boss? Angry words are written on your project. Words like "What is this?" "Where did you get this data?" "What am I to do with this information?" If so, just know that you are not alone. Half of the problems with poor performance are directly related to lack of information. Many of us will set out to do a task and have no idea what our boss expects or desires. One sure way to please your boss is to give him outcomes that are comparable to or better than what he would've done. This should give you a clue regarding my first strategy for Establishing Clear Expectations:

a. **Ask your boss for her opinions and/or ideas regarding ways the task could be completed.** Ask her for tips on how to approach or complete actions critical to the project's success.

b. **Get tips and strategies from staff members who have experience completing the task or activity.** Review their work and determine what processes or actions may be applicable to your project.

c. **Always discuss WHY the task/ project is important and WHO will benefit.**

d. **Ask what the finished product should look like.** This is for anything and everything you have questions about. If you know someone who has completed the project recently or is familiar with the requirements, talk to that person. Ask your boss (or client—same thing!) what, specifically, he liked about the previous projects or tasks (ask for a copy, if available). Then discuss how you could do something similar or better based on current priorities and strategies.

e. **Be clear regarding timelines and other parameters that could impact the success of the project.**

3. Develop a strategy

Now that you know exactly what is expected, you can create a strategy to achieve the outcome you desire. Consider the following:

a. **Do your research**. Take the time to learn what worked or didn't from past projects. If this kind of information is not available, solicit ideas from someone who has had success completing the task. (Note: Remember, people who help you may be doing so because they want some kind of reward or recognition. Be prepared to discuss the subject.) In short, be prepared to research the best methods for completing the task.

b. **Find help**. This may be the most overlooked step in organizations today. Most of us are hesitant to ask for help or assistance from our colleagues and associates. Determine who may have the knowledge and resources to assist you with parts of your project. In time, you will develop a consistent network of knowledgeable team members who will work with you to create success. Example: An MIT Specialist may be able to provide critical data to support a theory or project. The accountant can assist with budgetary projections for resources critical to a project's success.

c. **Determine the process**. Identify all the action steps required and then who will complete them, when they should be completed and how long it will take to complete.

d. **Estimate completion time and identify what resources will help facilitate your success.**

e. **Create a flowchart to monitor the progress of the task or project.**

f. **Continually discuss your progress with your boss or client**. Modify, if necessary.

4. Pay attention to detail

Are the measurements in feet or centimeters? Are the salary figures for full-time workers with benefits or for contractors? Know everything about your project.

5. Know what you are doing and always know the "rules"

Always work within established guidelines if they are not outdated or ineffective, and work with integrity.

6. Communicate the impact and benefits of your actions

Continually communicate the value that will be created from your actions. Provide specific data to support the impact of your efforts. Also, give credit to those who assisted your efforts. Remember the objectives you identified as performance targets and priorities for implementing the project. How have you met or exceeded expectations?

Sensible? Yes! Most importantly, these strategies will help you consistently perform at levels that exceed every expectation.

It is your fault. This is why you will be successful. Every job is an opportunity.

QUESTIONS TO THINK ABOUT

1. *Have you completed an assessment of your talents and skills?*

2. *List three things that you're great at!*

3. *Do you know what you're doing and what is expected from the project? If so, explain these to a colleague.*

4. *Have you explained HOW you'll complete the requested task? Have you discussed needed resources, timelines and contingencies that may hurt or hinder the project?*

5. *Have you created a sound working strategy for meeting and exceeding expectations?*

4

What Do They Know?

HOW OFTEN DO WE SEEK HELP, ADVICE OR COUNCIL? How many of us appreciate and respect the knowledge and experience of our colleagues, superiors and fellow staff members? The *what-do-they-know* mistake is committed by a great number of us who fail to recognize the talents, knowledge and abilities of those we work with. We fail to *learn what they know* and *use what they know* to our advantage. This is one of the most important lessons in life. *Everyone* knows something that we don't.

Think of the number of mistakes and errors we've made that could have been prevented if only we had asked someone for help or advice. Think of the times we worked extremely hard to complete a project, only to learn later that we could've completed it earlier, more easily and with less effort if we had sought help. I have known talented individuals who failed to reach their highest potential simply because they failed to secure the support of their colleagues.

This mistake is, once again, grounded in low self-esteem. A person with low self-esteem is often too embarrassed or too prideful to seek help from others. People with low self-esteem seldom respect or appreciate their coworkers—seeing them as adversaries instead of teammates. A by-product of low self-esteem is a failure to acknowledge the fact that people we work with have talent and ability.

As a young administrator who suffered from low self-esteem, I seldom had respect for the accomplishments of my coworkers. Why? Because I was concerned only about *my* welfare. I was always whining that *I* never got positive praise, never received quality assignments, never received recognition and rewards for all the work that I did. I never realized that perhaps others were getting recognition and rewards because they were actually doing something right. No way! It was always because they were liked more than I was, and (I was certain) they were a bunch of yes men/women who were always kissing up. I was determined *never* to be like them.

This approach alienated my colleagues and coworkers and left me unprotected and unsupported. Team members would argue with me and would seldom support any idea or plan that I presented. What could I expect when I never supported or took an interest in them? I was getting exactly what I was giving.

Your success is greatly impacted by the relationships and support networks you create. It will also be determined by how well you work with and relate to the other members of your team—yes, including your boss! Luckily, you got this book, and *I can give you some advice on ways you can win the support and appreciation of your team members.*

1. Observe Your Environment

The first key to achieving greater career success lies in understanding the *corporate culture* of your environment. Here are a few questions that will get you started.

- ✓ How are decisions made?
- ✓ Do managers have the ability to make free-will decisions or is there an approval process for everyone?
- ✓ Do people give input and feedback freely?
- ✓ Are people encouraged to take actions necessary to solve their own problems?
- ✓ Are people encouraged to try new ideas or concepts?
- ✓ How are team members encouraged to interact with one another?
- ✓ Does the boss insist that you bring problems to her prior to taking any action?
- ✓ Is there a high level of trust and professionalism?

2. Learn from the winners

Identify the people who always seem to get their proposals approved. Who are the people who seem to have the greatest influence on the team organization? Approach each of those team members and begin by letting the person know how much you appreciate him, especially his ability to get the job done. Be specific about what you like about the person. Next, ask for guidance or advice on areas that are of concern to you. We began this chapter discussing the benefits of council. You never have to make a mistake that has already been made by someone else. You can also proactively learn how to achieve your objectives by observing those who are achieving now. What methods are successful for them? What successful approaches are they using that may be applicable to you or your situation? What mistakes have they made that you'll want to avoid? Ask team members for advice for handling a difficult client, coworker or even the boss. You'll be surprised at the bond you'll begin to create with fellow team members.

3. Let Others In

One of the ways to get support from others is to allow them to have a stake in what you are proposing. Identify people within your organization who could help your proposal be successful. Tell them your idea and ask for their input. Let them know why you are asking (i.e., because of their expertise, knowledge or experience). Make a point to have regular feedback sessions on any project of interest. Anytime there's a new goal or project, don't take action until you've discussed it with your team or your colleagues. Tell them how their assistance to you will mean recognition or other benefits for them. Allow them to share in the glory or recognition if the project is successful. Again, this will go a long way in getting consistent support for your ideas. Let team members help you with the design and implementation, then share the glory with them. Everyone wins (especially you)!

4. Find a Coach or Mentor

This one move can have the greatest impact on your long-term success or failure. A mentor is a person with whom you form a relationship. The relationship can be similar to coach and player, student and teacher, or friend and advisor. This person should have experience and knowledge of your organization. A good mentor/coach will take time to meet with you to discuss issues, decisions and other important happenings within your organization. The coaching should serve two purposes: 1) help you understand how decisions are made and how organizational systems work; 2) show you how you can or could have responded in these situations in order to achieve a goal or an advantage. This relationship can open opportunities and strengthen your leadership and problem-solving skills. You'll also earn from a mentor or coach what it takes to become a successful leader. Here are a few steps that can help you find a coach/mentor.

- ✓ Find an experienced, successful leader or colleague who has many of the attributes and values you appreciate.

- ✓ Observe how this person responds to problems and challenges. Note the things she did or does that you like or appreciate.

- ✓ Take the person to lunch and discuss work. Focus on the "ways one can achieve success" within the organization. Tell him about your observations of them. Discuss what you appreciate about him.

- ✓ Sincerely ask this person to mentor or be a coach to you. Tell her that you have been looking for someone who could help you learn "the ropes" and other lessons necessary to achieve success.

- ✓ Get the person's thoughts on the idea and on your potential.

- ✓ Arrange a time to sit and set the parameters of the relationship (i.e., meeting times, feedback, projects and tasks to master). Ask him about his coaching approach or how he would like the relationship to work.

- ✓ Warning! If you do not deal well with honest assessments and constructive criticism, a mentor or coach would probably *not* work for you.

5. Build and Strengthen Relationships

Value the gifts and talents of your team members and colleagues. Be supportive of their ideas and projects. Don't publicly criticize or embarrass your colleagues. Offer advice on how they can achieve greater success. Here are a few more tips for building solid relationships with your colleagues:

a. **Be agreeable**. Arguing never gets other people to see things your way. Arguing just makes people angry, resentful and more determined to resist your way of thinking. Learn to be agreeable and easygoing. You don't have to challenge everyone. Resist the need to correct others or to "always be right." Use data and gentle (nonthreatening) language. Ask questions for greater understanding of their issues.

b. **Compliment and praise others**. We all feel unappreciated at some time in our lives. What's interesting is that most people at work feel unappreciated. If this is true, how do you think people will respond to you when you show appreciation? Have an attitude of gratitude. "Thank you" still works.

c. **Give attention**. Pay attention to others. Listen attentively. Repeat their words. Ask questions for clarification. Giving people your attention demonstrates respect and appreciation.

d. **Be a team player**. A team player is a person who puts the goals of the team ahead of individual or personal achievements. A team player works to enhance the effectiveness of the team. A team player provides feedback and guidance that's useful to team members. A team player helps team members achieve greater success via support, information or resources. Being a team player demonstrates a commitment to others that will surely be *reciprocated!*

e. **A rebel without a cause?** I have witnessed true conflict between colleagues that ripped relationships and organizations to the core. If you are angry, hostile or paranoid, you will create barriers and burn bridges, which could seriously hamper your chances for success. Are you building support systems or creating enemies?

Career success is impacted by the number of people working with you who can help you realize and achieve identified goals. You can have anything if you have enough talented people and resources behind you. You *never* win by judging or criticizing others. Zig Ziglar always said that we can get what we want from others by helping others get what they want! Begin by being good to others. Read Dale Carnegie's time-honored work and learn *"How to Win Friends and Influence People."*

Build a network of support from people you work for and with. These are the people who may lead you to future opportunities. A good relationship with them can help to expand and grow your career opportunities.

QUESTIONS OF CONCERN

1. Can you identify at least two people on your staff who you appreciate and respect? What makes them special?

2. What techniques are you learning from others that will help you be more successful in your current situation?

3. Have you selected a mentor? What are the qualities that you are looking for in a mentor?

4. What relationship strategies could be helpful in your current situation?

5. Who are the people at your job who could have the greatest positive impact on your immediate projects or long-range success goals?

5

What Plan?

THE ONLY WAY TO ACHIEVE THE LEVEL OF SUCCESS you deserve and desire is to work hard and plan for it. I once heard someone say, "You have to plan your work and work your plan." This was another one of my critical mistakes! I never had a *plan* for what I wanted to become, where I wanted to go or what I wanted to do. I took this same approach with me to every opportunity I received.

Too many of us simply go into a job or an opportunity unsure of what we want to do or accomplish. This is a critical mistake! There are two areas you must address when creating a plan: 1) What you desire to do and achieve in the current job you have; and 2) How the job can assist you in getting where you want to go.

With each opportunity I had, I neglected to create definitive plans regarding what I wanted to do and how I'd achieve it. I failed to talk with anyone about creating a success plan, a plan for achieving career success. I had a warped sense of what corporate life was about. Your life and your career require a plan.

To get you moving in the right direction, begin by asking yourself a number of questions relating to your career, such as:

- ✓ What do I want to do?
- ✓ What do I want to achieve in my career?
- ✓ What kind of work do I enjoy most?
- ✓ What skills must I master to be successful?
- ✓ How can my current job assist me in achieving my goals?
- ✓ Who can provide mentoring/coaching or recommendations for me?
- ✓ What's my next move? Where do I go from here (relating to job position)?

Success Keys for Current Job

Work to clarify your desires, goals and objectives. Know what you want to do, why it's important and how you'll attain a position in the area you desire. Understand the importance of relationships and how to develop and nurture them. We discussed strategies for this in earlier chapters. Next, understand processes and how to create value through productive systems. Keep improving and educating yourself as you prepare for your next great opportunity. Finally, create a plan for the allocation of your time and resources to achieve your goals while continuing to improve and grow professionally.

Developing a plan for success on your current job is really very simple. We discussed many of the steps necessary for achievement in Chapter 3. We'll reinforce many of those steps here. Begin by doing your research. *Know your company's philosophy, your boss's philosophy and the philosophy of your department or division.* Then focus on providing excellent services that are consistent with the philosophy and important to your customers/clients. Consider these steps as you develop your plan:

1. Identify Service Targets and Priorities

Meet with your boss and your customers to discuss their expectations and priorities for your products or services. Get a clear understanding of the performance expectations and priorities that will impact your organization. One idea is to conduct focus group discussions with your customers and colleagues.

✓ **Talk to your customers**. This is the first step in your success plan. Talk to customers about their expectations and needs. Ask customers for their top three service priorities relating to your operation. What do *you* need to do to meet their needs? This is always your first focus. (NOTE: Your boss is your first client.)

2. Build Your Service Team

Do you work with or lead a team, department or organization? Or are you responsible for achieving work goals alone? After learning what is desired or expected of you, you must determine what *resources* are available to assist you in achieving your objectives. Immediately begin to assess the resources you have:

✓ What are the strengths of your team or organization?

✓ Who are the outstanding performers within your team? How could they assist you in meeting the needs of your clients? What are their talents/skills?

✓ Who are the people you can count on to assist you, and what services will they provide?

✓ <u>If you lead the team.</u> Discuss the roles of each team member and the nature of his/her duties. Ensure that each member understands how his/her duties impact your organization or the client.

✓ <u>If you lead the team.</u> Evaluate the effectiveness of each member's activities, and get his/her ideas regarding how these activities could be improved or strengthened.

✓ Identify your suppliers, and communicate your expectations for services they provide you. How could they serve you better?

3. Improve Your Service Systems

What do you do for your clients/customers? What are the actions you implement regularly to meet your service objectives? What are the steps you need to take to address emergencies (power-outage, manpower shortage, computer glitches, etc.)? After you have identified and evaluated the members of your team, you must evaluate the *systems and processes* you use to provide the services your customers want. How well does your system work? (This may not excite you, but this is truly about the **bottom line**—your ability to produce.)

✓ Identify and assess those processes that are most critical for meeting the needs of your clients.

✓ Create quality monitors for assessing the effectiveness of your processes. How well do we do it? (It = steps we take to meet or exceed the expectations of our clients.)

✓ Continue to monitor, modify and upgrade your processes. Be proactive about eliminating those steps that are unnecessary or ineffective. How could your system be improved?

4. Communicate

Make a habit to always communicate your intentions and desires to those you are serving and those working with you.

- ✓ Communicate to your clients about what they can expect you to do to solve their problems.
- ✓ Talk to your staff and team members about your needs and expectations—or what they can do to help your team achieve targeted goals. Discuss what activities you'd like to have implemented.
- ✓ Communicate to team members the roles they'll play and outcomes you're expecting. Discuss contingencies and strategies for dealing with potential problems.
- ✓ Let staff and team members know your expectations. They need to know what success "looks like."
- ✓ Finally, on a consistent basis, let people know:
  - how the job will be completed
  - outcomes they can expect
  - how to access your system
  - who they can call when there are problems
  - when they can expect completion or delivery

5. Network and Collaborate

What really surprises me is how few of us value the help, support and opinions of others. I never concerned myself with "who I knew." I felt my knowledge and talent would take me to the top. Had I developed more friends and contacts, I could've achieved so much more. How? More *support*, more *assistance* and more *help* always means more **sustained success**. Form liaisons with professionals who have your drive, interests and determination. Join professional clubs and associations to stay up to date on the latest and best practices being used by others in your field or profession.

By *creating partnerships with others*, you develop skills in team building, motivation, communication and leadership. Most importantly, you learn strategies for building consensus, negotiating and for motivating people to move in a certain direction. Finally, you may actually *enjoy the friendships you create*.

It's WHO You Know and WHO Knows You

Another powerful reason to continue to strengthen relationships is directly related to your job search. We have more success when our team members respect and support us. This support is even more beneficial when you are looking for another job, a promotion or an expansion of your current duties. Most people forget that the majority of top executives *did not* learn about their opportunities from the newspaper or even an on-line job site. Most top-level executives learned about their current jobs (and even received recommendations) from other people! The best jobs are not advertised in the newspaper. And do you really think you're going to get a great opportunity without a great recommendation (hopefully from someone the employer knows and trusts)? So, there are even more reasons to build strong work relationships.

Commit to service. Commit to a plan. Then create a system that will allow you to achieve the things you want. Don't forget, people can and will help you get it done if they know what you want, desire and expect. Also, always remember to recognize and reward others for their help or assistance.

Your plan should cover what you want to do and where you'd like to go within your career, including the titles (CEO, Vice President, Department Director) you'd like to achieve. This will virtually *guarantee* your success. Why? Because the great majority of professionals are skating by the seats of their pants! You'll consistently outperform any competitor when you have a plan! Create your plan today.

QUESTIONS TO THINK ABOUT

1. *Have you identified what you really want to do with your career, your future, even your current job opportunity?*

2. *Have you written your goals? Write out your goals for the next two years. Break down the process to include goals for your professional life. Also include educational goals, physical fitness goals, relationship goals, financial goals and spiritual goals. Make your goal statements S.M.A.R. T.:*

   Specific

   Measurable

   Actionable

   Realistic

   Time-Specific

3. *Have you identified the service priorities for your operation?*

4. *Have you addressed how you'll achieve what's expected of you and your team?*

5. *Have you created a plan for building relationships that could impact your future?*

6

Study? Why? I'm Already Good!

THE FIRST PIECE OF ADVICE YOUR MENTOR MAY GIVE YOU could be to keep getting better! Your overall success will be impacted by your commitment to excellence and becoming a lifelong learner. A critical mistake many professionals make is assuming that they now know it all. They assume things will stay the way they are right now. It's also not surprising to know that most of us are creatures of habit and have difficulty dealing with change and the unfamiliar.

You may be out of school. You may have had some success. You may feel that you have seen it all and have it all under control. You may have several years of experience, but as a professional (who truly desires success), **the learning has only just begun!**

Many professionals and managers get stuck on one approach, process, procedure or system that is familiar, comfortable and successful. The problem with the one-way approach of doing anything is that when the environment, people or priority changes, we are *slow in adjusting* to meet the *new demands*. As a result, many opportunities are lost. Change is the only certainty in life! Consistently late responses will have you rushing to catch up. Playing catch-up is never good in business.

The only way to ensure that your future will be as successful as it is currently is to commit to a process of continual learning. Life in the real world is fast, ever-changing and unpredictable. Your success in this world requires you to be just as fast and flexible in your responses. Begin a **Total Quality Assessment** of yourself. Identify ways you can improve your effectiveness. Here's how this can be done:

1. Professional Competence

Always start by assessing how well you consistently achieve your personal and professional goals. Have you outlined your professional goals and objectives, including how you will achieve them? Also, review your organizational priorities, as we discussed earlier. You should also get a feel for where your profession is heading. What will the future job market look like for people in your profession? Create a "professional compe-tence" improvement plan.

a. **Communication (written and oral).** No one trait can aid your success or fuel your failure more quickly than your ability to communicate. This is your greatest resource for getting things done and getting what you want. It's necessary to *sell yourself*, and your ideas, as a professional. You can improve your communication skills by taking classes or seminars or listening to self-help tapes and CDs. I took a communications course at a community college while working a residency at the Hines VA Hospital outside of Chicago. I joined a local chapter of Toastmasters to improve my presentation and speaking skills. The key is for you to keep improving these skills. Computer skills are critical for effective communication. The use of e-mail will continue its explosive growth. So continue to improve your typing and editing skills, as well.

b. **Ability to work well with others.** No matter what you do or how good you are at doing it, most of you will still have a reliance on others to complete your assignments and tasks. Your ability to work well with others and as a member of a team is so important that most top managers have listed it as a critical characteristic they look for when hiring a manager (according to a survey completed by the American Management Association—interviewing 300 top executives). So, be kind, patient and accepting of others (again, we discussed this earlier). There are many ways to improve this skill, and there are many books, CDs, workshops and seminars on the subject.

c. **Organization/administrative skills.** If you can get through administrative red tape and create a process with fewer steps for greater efficiency, you are valued! Almost everything requires an administrative process. Learn these processes. Learn how to get needed resources. Learn how to modify your systems to achieve your objectives. Create contingency plans to deal with the unexpected. Like my old bosses, Al Pate and John DeNardo, used to say, "Pay attention to details, details, details!" Finally, keep your eye peeled for new innovations and ideas that can make your processes even better.

d. **Emotional stability and confidence.** This is one area that can cause great anxiety, unhappiness and stress. Work on always maintaining a professional demeanor. Keep your composure and think before speaking. You may find yourself in difficult, often hostile, situations at work. Remember that angry reactions toward others are never beneficial to you (or valued by your employer). Don't pass blame or make excuses. Simply discuss the things you can control and fix the problem. Work on assertive communication techniques. Read and listen to information that builds your self-esteem. Authors such as Jack Canfield, Brian Tracy and Deepak Chopra emphasize a number of stress-reducing strategies in many of their writings and audio programs. Use self-talk (or affirmations) to help you stay focused and relaxed. Don't take things too personally or too seriously. Always be supportive of team members and your leaders.

e. **Join professional associations and organizations.** If you are really serious about achieving success in a given field, your first order of business should be to join a professional organization/association. These organizations will be extremely valuable to you. They keep you abreast of the latest trends, concerns, technologies and benchmarks within your field. You'll network with and meet people within the field who may turn you on to employment possibilities. You'll attend workshops and seminars to enhance your skills and professional competence. As a hospital administrator, I was a member of the American College of Healthcare Executives. My hospital was a member of the American Hospital Association. As a speaker and consultant, I was a member of the National

Speakers Association. Find the professional organizations that meet your needs and join. P.S.—Don't forget alumni associations from your alma mater. These relationships can prove to be extremely valuable to you.

How would you rate yourself in these areas? (Also, ask others to rate you if you desire diverse opinions):

Professional Trait	(Rating)	1	2	3	4
Communication					
Organization					
Ability to Work Well					
Emotional/Self-Esteem					
Organizations/Associations					

After you identify what you do well and what you don't do so well, you'll have a foundation upon which to build an improvement plan. Your improvement efforts should begin with those skills or traits that can have the greatest impact on your ability to create value. Develop a strategy for improving your skills in this critical area, then work into other areas.

Begin right where you are. Find and network with people within your organization who seem to make it happen. Learn from their strategies (and mistakes), then create your own strategies.

2. Become a Master Technician

Learn every aspect of what's expected of you professionally. Become an expert in your field, a "Master Technician." Determine your effectiveness. Focus on finding solutions that allow you to increase your effectiveness. Think outside the box and keep getting better. Learn how to alter and modify your approaches for optimal effectiveness. Use every experience to grow your skills. This is the key to your long-term success. Soon you'll become virtually unstoppable.

3. Find Five Better Ways

Keep looking for ways to get better and to be better. I learned of a concept called "Three Better Ways." The idea was to think of some area of your life and think of three ways you may be able to improve it. Of course, the idea stayed with me, and now I'm using it. I truly believe that there is no limit to how much better we could be if only we'd make self-improvement a way of life. Assess the areas of your life: job/career, work relationships, personal relationships, your financial growth and your physical and spiritual health. As you think about the many facets that make up your "total package," ask yourself, "How many ways could I be better in this area?" Take out a sheet of paper and brainstorm responses for each category. Within a matter of minutes you'll begin having revelations regarding ways you can be more successful within a given area. Over the next few days, continue to think of ways you can improve until you have at least **five ways** you can improve in each category. Now that you have a direction, let the improvements begin!

Improving keeps you at the top of your game and launches you toward your goals. Remember, every experience provides learning. You'll be amazed at what each day will teach you.

QUESTIONS

1. *What are my greatest professional strengths?*

2. *Where could I improve? What area requires the most or immediate attention?*

3. *What improvements can have the greatest impact on my ability to achieve my objectives?*

4. *Have I discussed* Where/What/How *I can improve with my boss or direct report?*

5. *Have I created a strategy for improving my skills?*

6. *Have I completed the "Five Better Ways" exercise?*

7

Who Cares?

A POOR ATTITUDE IS EASY TO RECOGNIZE and hard to forget. A poor attitude is often prevalent with poor performers. A critical mistake is feeling that "it just doesn't matter" what you do or what you think or that no one is paying attention to you. Many people feel that their indifference or lack of caring is justified by some past wrong or lack of support from the company. Let's make this perfectly clear: **the kiss of death to your career happens when you project a feeling that says, "I don't care."**

How often have you heard people say things like these?

- ✓ They don't pay me enough to do this job.
- ✓ I couldn't care less what happens here.
- ✓ Hey, it's no concern to me one way or the other.
- ✓ This is management's baby; let them worry about it.
- ✓ I'm not volunteering for anything!

✔ What do I care? I've only got one more year until retirement!

✔ This job means nothing to me.

Every career has many ups and downs. There will be challenges that you'll win and many that you'll lose. Some of you will even face challenges that will be or seem unfair. Regardless, it is your responsibility to always respond like a professional. Your responses will build or destroy your reputation and the overall perception of your value. Your boss, staff, team members and members of the executive team will be watching to see how well you handle stress, change(s), disappointments and difficulties. Mental toughness plays a critical role in building others' perception of you as a *seasoned professional*, ready to tackle any challenge. Demonstrate toughness, and your focus on improving will provide you with an unshakable foundation of excellence.

Here are a few truths *all* professionals should remember:

1. EVERYONE has failed and has experienced setbacks. Ask any CEO!

2. BAD THINGS will happen to you just as they do to everyone.

3. Success is always determined by YOUR RESPONSE(S) to the bad things.

4. Failure is always TEMPORARY!

Re-read these truths and commit them to memory so you can have them when "bad things" begin to happen to you! Now you are ready to keep growing and evolving as a professional. You'll only get better and better with each experience.

1. Maintain Your Focus

Keep your mind on your job and your priorities. Review your approaches and work processes for effectiveness. Modify, change or eliminate those actions that are not getting you the results you desire. The key is to learn and grow from your mistakes—not repeat them! Also, remember that most people you deal with at work are thinking of one thing: getting what *they* want. Keep your focus on helping them achieve their objectives, and your value will continue to rise. We discussed a few of these approaches in earlier chapters, but the information still applies. If you can't control it or impact it, then forget it! Focus on what you can control.

a. Keep lines of communication open and positive.

b. Let people know what you can do and will do for them.

c. Get others involved in the process. Ask for suggestions, and recognize valuable input from others.

d. Keep your focus on valued outcomes and solutions that will create those outcomes.

2. Control Your Emotions/Anger

There is never a need to speak negatively about your problems to others within your organization. Never publicly criticize your boss, team members, the organization or the organization's goals and direction. I wouldn't recommend it in private conversations either. What good will it do if the conversation is designed to stimulate ideas or solutions? Sure, everyone whines about the job now and then (and to this day, many of them are still "labeled" as whiners). The question that must always be at the forefront of your thinking is, Will this comment actually fix, repair or eliminate the problem? If you answer yes, then speak. Otherwise, just relax.

Also, avoid arguing or giving strong opinions to team members if these have little to do with solving the problem. Please understand, I want your focus to always be on one thing: ways you can create outcomes that are desired, respected and valued by others. Nothing else really matters! Remember the Law of Reciprocation, or the Law of Sowing and Reaping. Criticisms we give to others are quickly returned to us. If you are constantly critical of others or the organization, you will soon develop a reputation as a whiner or pessimist, and your opinions will be devalued. Plus, people will tend to stay away from you or become defensive around you. There's a better way:

a. **In a disagreement or conflict with another, try to see your adversary as an "honorable staff member" who wants what's best for the company or organization.** Do not take criticisms personally. Try to express appreciation for the other person's idea (even though yours is better). You may begin your debate with, *"I can appreciate Mr. Johnson's desire to improve our effectiveness. However, I believe there may be more cost-effective ways to proceed. Here are my thoughts...."*

b. **Never argue.** You'll never win an argument. Try always to find "points of agreement," then build your conversation from there. Points of agreement will bring into focus things you have in common and could serve as a springboard to greater agreements.

c. **Manage your mouth.** Sarcastic remarks can be taken out of context. Jokes are not always funny or appropriate.

"Popping off" shows a lack of maturity and intelligence. Yes! You've guessed it! I've been guilty of these stupid mistakes, too! Speak in ways that enhance value and win cooperation from peers. Keep the communication positive, upbeat and solution-focused.

d. **Learn from every experience.** Things happen for a reason. Every time you experience human conflict, use the experience to improve your effectiveness with others. Each negative experience provides valuable lessons regarding how people think. Keep getting better. (You know, from the previous chapter.)

e. **Ask the right questions.** In his book *The Question Behind the Question,* Jim Miller says that people fail to accept personal responsibility for their actions because they fail to ask the right questions of themselves. The right questions will have the answers for you. For example, instead of asking, "Why doesn't my boss give me good work projects?" the question could be, "What can I do to grow my boss's confidence in me?" This question places the focus and responsibility right back in your lap. So you focus on being empowered instead of being a victim. Always keep your focus on what you can control—your attitude and your actions. Ask How and What questions (e.g., How can I improve this relationship? or What can I do to make this situation better?).

3. Think Outside The Box

Yes. I'm very serious. If you are starting to feel that you can't win at a job and that you may stop caring, it's probably because you are not experiencing the success you may be accustomed to. If this is the case, then you are a perfect candidate to begin examining ways to get out of the box! We *play* this professional game the way we are *taught* to play it. Well, if you're not achieving the success you want by playing by the rules, then perhaps it's time to examine the rules you are playing by. Examine and assess how you do business. If you find you are not having success, then it may be time to get out of the box. Free yourself from those old rules and start operating under new or different and, perhaps, more effective rules. There are many formulas for thinking outside the box:

a. **Always more than one way.** As you review your situation(s), ask yourself, "How many ways could I do this?" Review your options and come up with new strategies.

b. **Learn from other/outside sources.** There are organizations everywhere that are doing things right and doing the right things. Study successful organizations and leaders and learn from them.

c. **Learn from history.** What worked in the past that may work again today?

d. **Brainstorm responses with your team.** This is an excellent way to get and keep everyone involved and thinking.

e. **Use temporary solutions.** Can't come up with a permanent fix to your problem? It's okay. Create a temporary solution that can keep your operation moving ahead until a long-term solution can be agreed on.

CONSIDER THIS

1. *When challenged or in conflict, I resist the temptation to defend myself or attack the other person.*

2. *I don't criticize my organization, coworkers or management.*

3. *I bring an optimistic attitude to work with me.*

4. *When in conflict, I stay solutions-focused and in control.*

5. *I am constantly looking for ways get out of the box to find new solutions to problems.*

8

I'm Too Good for This Job!

ONE OF THE SADDEST ASPECTS OF THE HUMAN CONDITION is the tendency we have of overvaluing ourselves and our performances. Even when things are not going well within our professional lives, most of us will look outside of ourselves for the causes of those problems. It's always what someone else is doing to us that creates our problems. This approach helps to create the eighth and final mistake. People who feel that they're *too good* or *overqualified* for their jobs are forgetting the most important factor for long-term career success—appreciation!

How many of us sit back and really give thanks for the *opportunity* to work? Yes, I know that you are valuable. I know that you are great at what you do. However, none of us would be at our jobs today were it not for having the **opportunity to perform.**

Now this does not mean you should settle for having any position or doing anything. No, in fact if you have talent in other areas, or if you are not being used to your fullest capacity, then you should seek other or greater challenges. No one should stay in a job that does not challenge, stimulate and grow his/her skills and abilities. The problem comes when we focus only on "how good" we are. When this happens, we are at risk to stop performing. We cannot consistently create value for others when we think only of ourselves. When we stop performing and producing, the perception of our value begins to drop. This often leads to missed opportunities for increased responsibilities or even promotions we may desire. **Avoid this mistake!**

1. Appreciate the Opportunity

Remember that you asked to be hired, and someone (perhaps your boss) gave you this opportunity. Perhaps the job is not all that you expected, but at least you got the opportunity to try it. Appreciate this fact and keep your interest and intensity at a high level. Always begin any journey by appreciating where you are and mastering the job functions. If you continually do it here, the odds are you'll have the opportunity to perform somewhere else, maybe in the place or job you truly desire.

2. Experience Works to Your Advantage

Having this job provides you with opportunities for growth and learning. This can help you to land other jobs and opportunities. What are you learning about yourself and your work style? What are you learning about your ability to handle pressure, coordinate tasks, deal with criticisms or lead others? Remember, *keep getting better.*

3. Be Passionate

Everything in your life is impacted by your state of mind. If you are passionate about your career opportunities, then you'll never have a bad job. Every job will lead to greater opportunities. Passionate people tend to find the good in any circumstance, and they seem to excel when others are ready to quit. Why? Because passion provides a number of undeniable benefits to the person who has it. These benefits include:

a. **Increased focus and intensity.** Your mind is alive and awake when you are passionate. You can't wait to start working on your project or on your daily routine. You're excited and in tune.

b. **Greater creativity and problem-solving.** Passion stimulates your mind. A fast mind means finding solutions to problems more quickly and more efficiently.

c. **Greater stamina, strength and determination.** People with passion don't give up, and they don't get tired. They have the ability to outperform others and finish difficult tasks. Passion provides a boost of energy that enhances your overall ability to perform at higher levels longer.

d. **Greater job enjoyment and patience.** Passionate people don't sweat the small stuff! They seem at ease and are seldom rattled by the incompetence of others or when problems arise.

4. Enjoy the Experience!

This is perhaps the simplest (yet best) advice I can give you. There are too many people in this world who don't know how to enjoy their lives or their work. They whine and complain about their situations and forget that everything is a choice! If you really want your life to be different or better, then make up your mind and change it. The truth is that we are responsible for our own happiness. How do we enjoy the experience? Simply remind yourself every day how much you are enjoying your work. Remind yourself of the value you are creating for others and the good you bring. Remember that how you work reflects a certain set of values; your level of Personal Excellence. And don't forget about the people you work with, learn from and have fun with.

Most importantly, remember that even though you're at work, this is your life. The time you spend at work will never be recouped. We spend over 60 percent of our adult lives at work. You're not just working; you're living! So let work reflect how you live. A colleague, mentor and friend of mine, Steve Gilliland, wrote a book that echoes this philosophy: *Enjoy The Ride.* In it, he reminds us that our "state of mind" creates success or failure, heartache or joy while on life's ride. Steve would say, "Are you Passionate?" So be determined to live with energy, passion and high expectations. You deserve the best, and you'll have it all— a tremendous career, greater prosperity and a happier life—if you will only *Avoid The Eight Critical Mistakes.* Good luck!

REMEMBER—SUCCESS IS YOUR FAULT!
YOU ARE NOW READY. ALL THE SUCCESS TO YOU!

Don't stop here. Read the book again, then pass it on—or tell at least two friends about it!

Acknowledgments

IT HAS BEEN A LONG TIME COMING. For a while it seemed like I'd never get this book out, but it's finally here. I want to thank those around me who've assisted me in a variety of ways.

First, though I haven't always been the best father and husband, I thank my family for their patience, love and support—thank you, Thea, Eli and Noah. Hopefully things will settle down a little, and there'll be less stress from the old man.

I want to thank my brother Larry Gordon for his guidance and advice on anything in life. Hey KK!! **I thank my mother,** Amy Gordon, for hanging in there under very difficult circumstances and still standing strong in love and faith. I love you, Mom! My father is no longer here—I'm sorry it took so long, Dad. I never meant to leave you out of my earlier work. Thanks, George Gordon! Hang in there, my brothers: Dar, Bruce and Kell-Dog!

I'd also like to thank a few of my close colleagues who assisted in reading my drafts and making great suggestions. I appreciate you all, and let me know if I can ever be of assistance for any project you may have in the future. Thank you, Steve Gilliland, Veronica Allen, Arquila Todd and Vickie Norman. Thank you for all of your support and assistance—it's finally done!

Thanks to good friends who have always been available, even if it's just to talk. Thank you, Craig Owens (for being my best friend in life—through thick and thin), Sammy B. Anderson, Jacoby Jackson, Scotty Allen, Melvin Washington and Todd Caliva—the best Hospital Administrator in Texas!

Most importantly, thank you to all of my former bosses who put up with my incompetence all these years and who were witnesses to my personal mistakes (and growth). You all were fantastic and taught me much about corporate and organizational success. I respect and appreciate each of you! Thanks again, Al Pate (George Rodman and John DeNardo), Wayne Ogburn, Dr. Anderson, Colonel F. R. Stevens, Mary Combs, Miss Abby and Larry Wallace.

Thank you, God, for keeping me strong, healthy and determined to make a difference. This will be a great year!

About Eric Gordon

Eric Gordon enjoys being a consultant. He's spent the last 12 years of his life training executives, managers and employees from over 100 organizations throughout the United States, Canada, Australia and Great Britain. A graduate of Michigan State University, Mr. Gordon received his masters in Health Service Administration from George Washington, University. He served as a Captain in the United States Air Force - Medical Services Corps and has over 10 years experience as a health care executive.

To contact G. Eric Gordon regarding speaking engagements, or to purchase his books, please visit his web site at www.gericgordon.com or call 1-972-922-3549.

BOOKS BY G. ERIC GORDON

"Avoiding the 8 Critical Mistakes ...That Will Short-Circuit Your Career"

"Common Sense Solutions for Success"